VOL. 42

HAL•LEONARD®
DRUM PLAY-ALONG

EASY ROCK SONGS

AUDIO ACCESS INCLUDED

PLAYBACK+
Speed • Pitch • Balance • Loop

To access audio visit:
www.halleonard.com/mylibrary

Enter Code
5980-1592-0818-1251

ISBN 978-1-4950-2837-3

HAL•LEONARD®
CORPORATION
7777 W. BLUEMOUND RD. P.O. BOX 13819 MILWAUKEE, WI 53213

Visit Hal Leonard Online at
www.halleonard.com

EASY ROCK SONGS

CONTENTS

All Right Now

Words and Music by Andy Fraser and Paul Rodgers

wait ____ or hes - i - tate. _ Let's move be - fore they raise the park - ing

Chorus

rate." Ow! ____ All right now. _ Ba - by, it's all _

____ right ____ now. _____ All right

now. _ Ba - by, it's all _____ right _ now. _____ Whoa. _

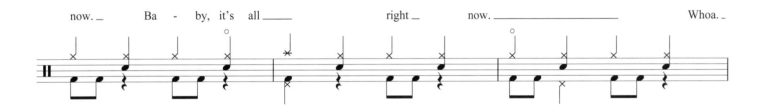

_____ Let me tell ya now. Oo, ah.

Verse

2. I took her home _____ to my

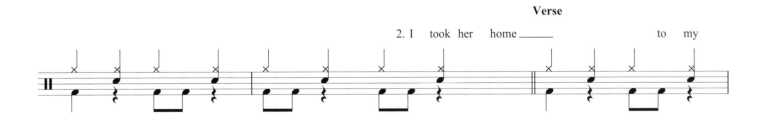

place, _ watch - ing ev - 'ry move on her face. _ She said,

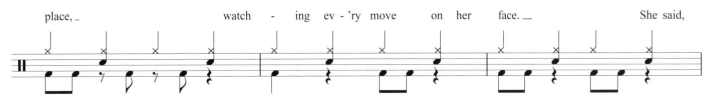

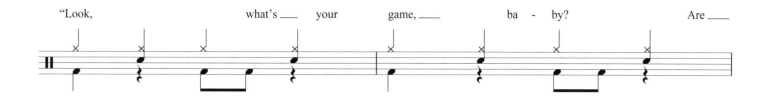

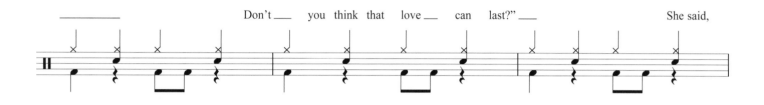

Chorus

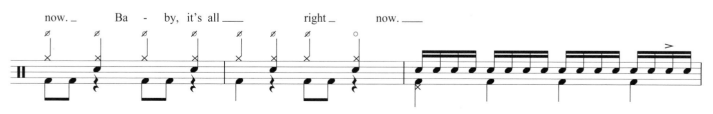

Yeah, it's all right now.

Oh. _____

Oh, yeah. __

Bridge

Ow!

Let me tell you all a - bout ___ it now. Ow! Yeah.

Verse

3. Took her home ____ to my

place, _ watch - ing ev - 'ry move on her face. __ She said,

Ba - by, it's all _____ right.   Yeah.

All   right   now. _____   Ba - by, ba - by, ba - by, it's all

right. ___   All,   all ___ right   now.   Yeah, ___

it's all right, it's all right, it's all   right,   yeah, huh.   All   right   now. _

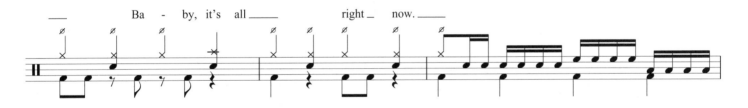

___   Ba - by, it's all _____   right _ now. _____

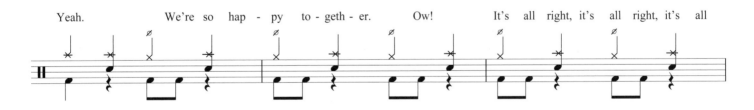

Yeah.   We're so hap - py to - geth - er.   Ow!   It's all right, it's all right, it's all

right. _   Ev -'ry - thing's all right.   Yeah.   Woo! _____

Free time

rit.

Fight for Your Right
(To Party)

Words and Music by Rick Rubin, Adam Horovitz and Adam Yauch

Intro
Moderately fast ♩ = 134

Kick it!

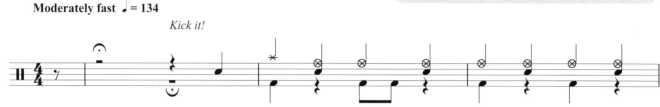

1. You

Verse

wake up late for school, man, you don't wan - na go.
2., 3. *See additional lyrics*

2nd time, substitute Fill 1

You ask your mom, "Please?" but she still says, "No!"

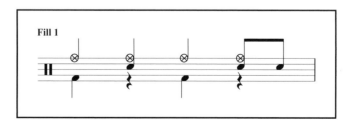

You missed two class-es and no home-work, but your teach-er preach-es class like you're some kind of jerk.

To Coda ⊕
Chorus

You got-ta fight _____ for your right _____ to par-ty. _____

|1. 2. Your

Interlude

You got-ta fight. _

Guitar Solo

Interlude

Outro

Par - ty. ___

___

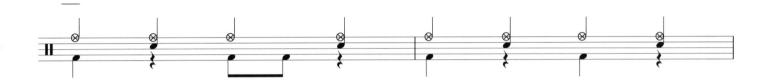

Par - ty. _____

___

Additional Lyrics

2. Your pops caught you smoking, man, he says, "No way."
   That hypocrite smokes two packs a day.
   Man, livin' at home is such a drag.
   Now your mom threw away your best porno mag. Bust it.

3. "Don't step out of this house if that's the clothes you're gonna wear."
   "I'll kick you outta my home if you don't cut that hair."
   Your mom busted in and said, "What's that noise?"
   Oh, mom, you're just jealous, it's the Beastie Boys!

Gimme Some Lovin'

Words and Music by Steve Winwood, Muff Winwood and Spencer Davis

LEGEND

Drummer: Pete York

Intro

Moderately ♩ = 147

Play 10 times

Hey!

Verse

1. Well, my tem - p'ra - ture's ris - ing and my feet left the floor. _

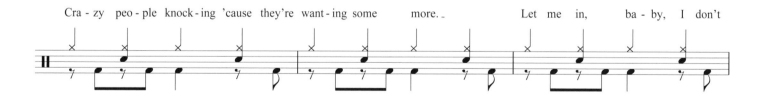

Cra - zy peo - ple knock - ing 'cause they're want - ing some more. _ Let me in, ba - by, I don't

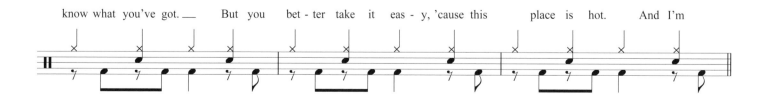

know what you've got. _ But you bet - ter take it eas - y, 'cause this place is hot. And I'm

Pre-Chorus

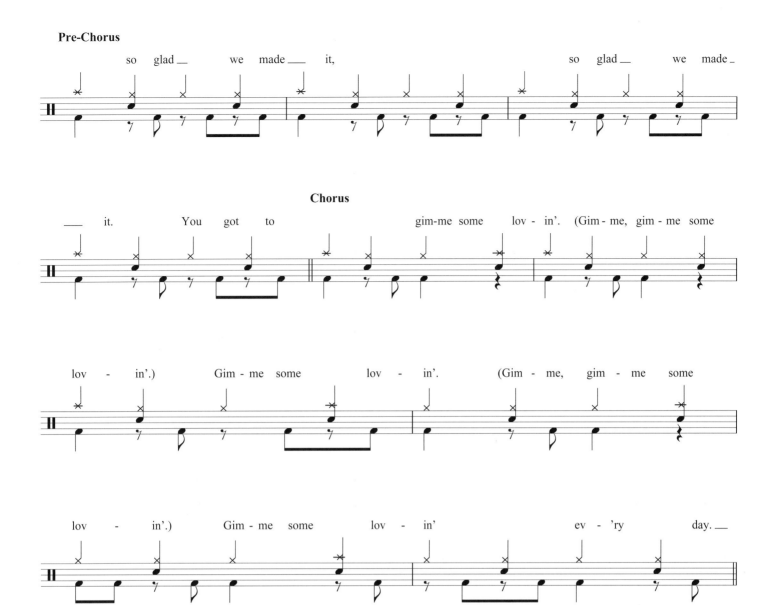

Chorus

Interlude

Hey!

Verse

2. Well, I feel _____ so good, _ ev - 'ry - thing is get - ting hot. _ You

bet - ter take it eas - y, 'cause the place is on fire. _ Been a hard day, _ and I

had some work to do. _ We made it, ba - by, and it hap-pened to you. And I'm

Pre-Chorus

so glad _ we made _ it, so glad _ we made _

Chorus

_ it. You got to gim - me some lov -

in'. (Gim - me, gim - me some lov - in'.) Gim-me some lov - in'. (Gim - me, gim - me some lov - in'.)   Gim - me   some   lov - in'   ev - 'ry   day. ⎯

Interlude

Hey!   3. Well, I   feel ⎯

Verse

⎯ so   good, ⎯   ev - 'ry - thing is get - ting hot. ⎯   You   bet - ter take it   eas - y, 'cause the

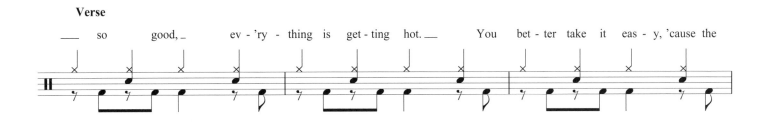

place is on   fire. ⎯   It's   been a   hard   day; ⎯ noth - in'   went   too good.   Now I'm

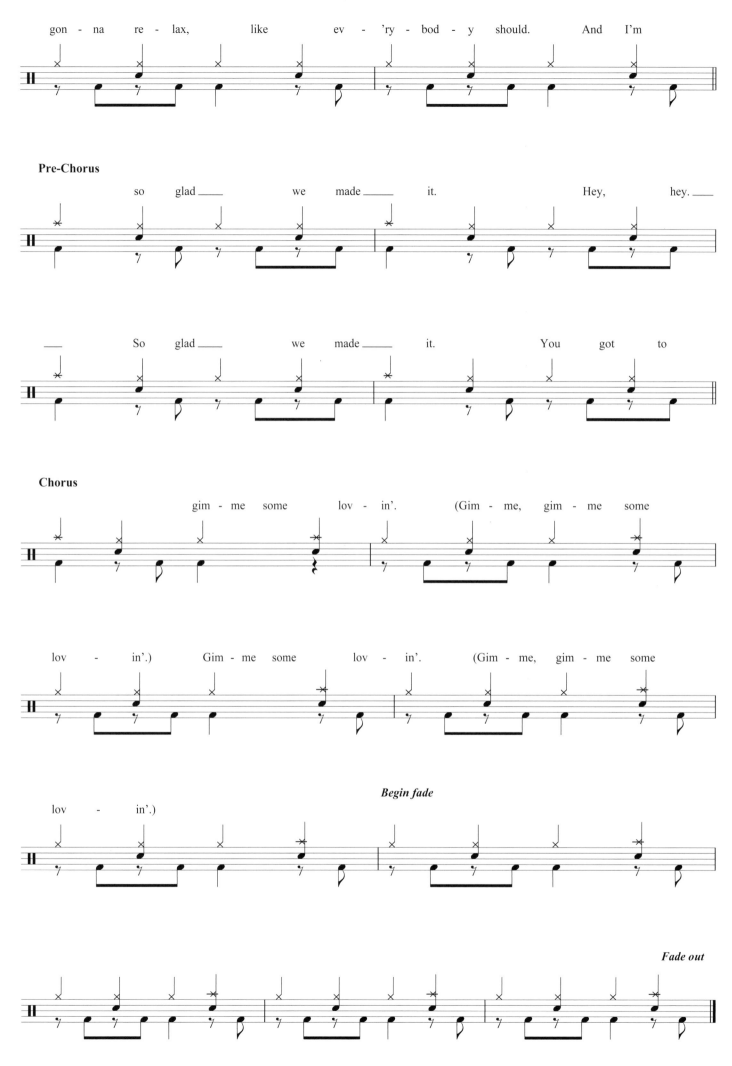

Sharp Dressed Man

Words and Music by Billy F Gibbons, Dusty Hill and Frank Lee Beard

Intro
Moderate Rock ♩ = 124

Play 3 times

𝄋 **Verse**
2nd & 3rd times, substitute Fill 1

1. Clean shirt, _____ new shoes, _____ and I don't know where I am
2., 3. *See additional lyrics*

go - in' to. _____ Silk suit, _____ black tie, _____

To Coda 2 ⊕

Chorus

I don't need a rea - son why. _____ They come run - nin' just as

Fill 1

fast as they can, __ 'cause ev - 'ry girl's __ cra - zy 'bout a sharp dressed man. __

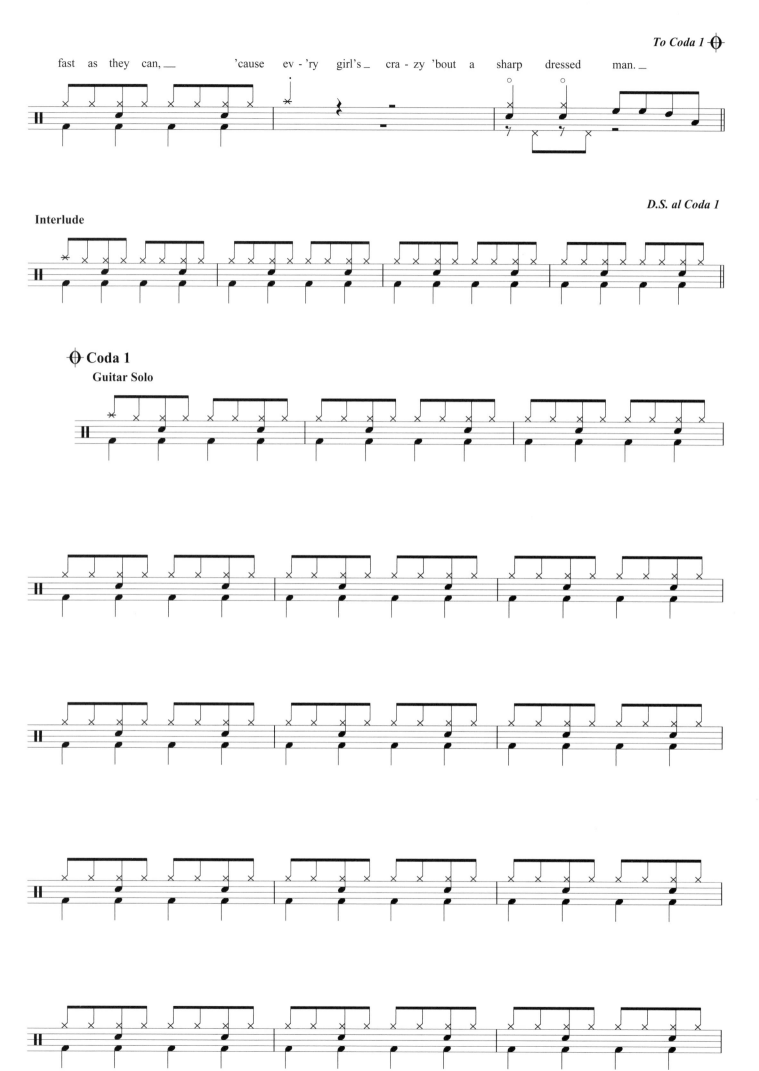

D.S. al Coda 1

Interlude

⊕ **Coda 1**

Guitar Solo

Interlude

D.S. al Coda 2

⊕ Coda 2

Chorus

Look-in' for love. _   They come run-nin' just as   fast as they can, _   'cause

Outro-Guitar Solo

ev - 'ry girl's _ cra - zy 'bout a   sharp   dressed   man. _

Play 3 times

Begin fade

Fade out

Additional Lyrics

2. Gold watch, diamond ring,
   I ain't missin' not a single thing.
   Cuff links, stick pin,
   When I step out I'm gonna do you in.

3. Top coat, top hat,
   An' I don't worry 'cause my wallet's fat.
   Black shades, white gloves,
   Lookin' sharp, lookin' for love.

Highway to Hell

Words and Music by Angus Young, Malcolm Young and Bon Scott

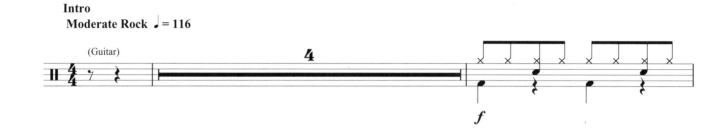

Intro
Moderate Rock ♩ = 116

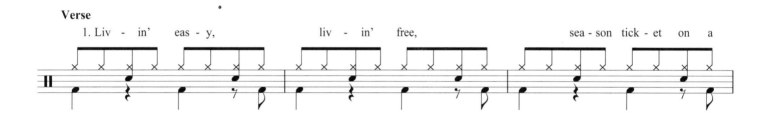

Verse

1. Liv - in' eas - y, liv - in' free, sea - son tick - et on a

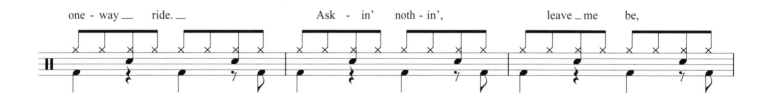

one - way __ ride. __ Ask - in' noth - in', leave __ me be,

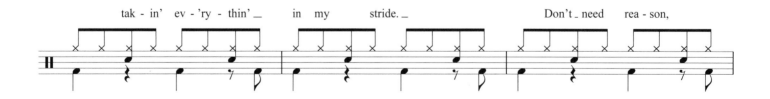

tak - in' ev - 'ry - thin' __ in my stride. __ Don't __ need rea - son,

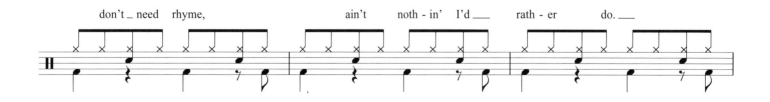

don't __ need rhyme, ain't noth - in' I'd __ rath - er do. __

Go - in' down,   par - ty time, __   my friends are gon - na

be there too. __   Yeah.   I'm on the high   - way   to hell. __

Chorus

__   On the high   - way   to hell. __

High   - way   to hell. __   I'm on the high   - way   to hell. __

__   2. No __ stop signs,   speed _ lim - it,

Verse

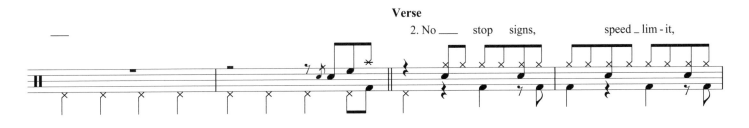

no - bod - y's gon - na slow me __ down. __   Like _ a wheel, _

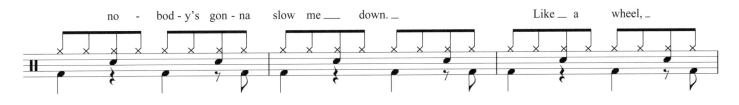

gon - na spin it;   no - bod - y's gon - na mess me a - round. __

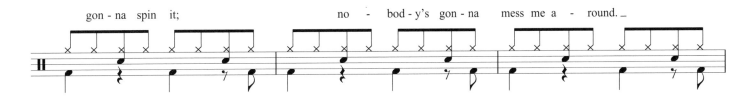

Hey Sa - tan,   pay'n' _ my dues,   play - in' in a

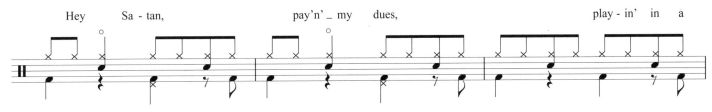

Outro-Chorus

Learning to Fly

Words and Music by Tom Petty and Jeff Lynne

Intro
Moderately ♩ = 116

1. Well, I

Verse

start - ed out ____   down a dirt - y road, ____

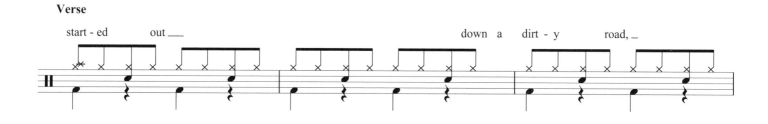

start - ed ____ out _

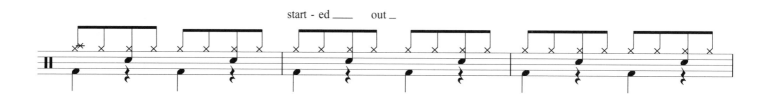

all a - lone. _   And the sun went down _

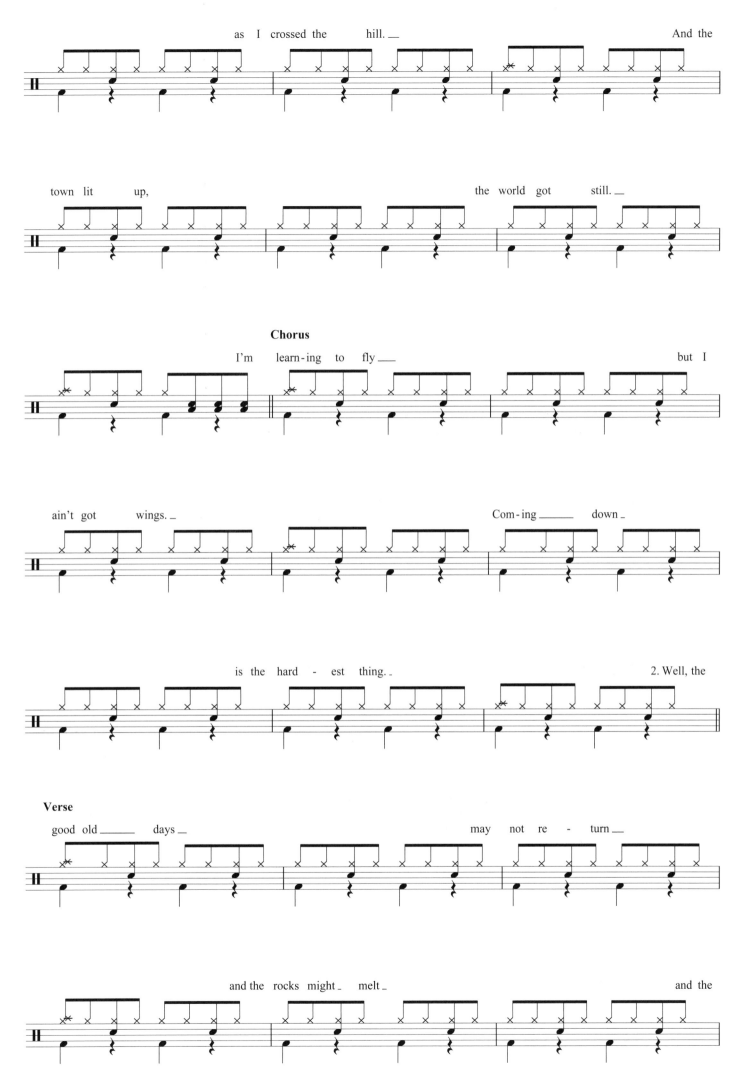

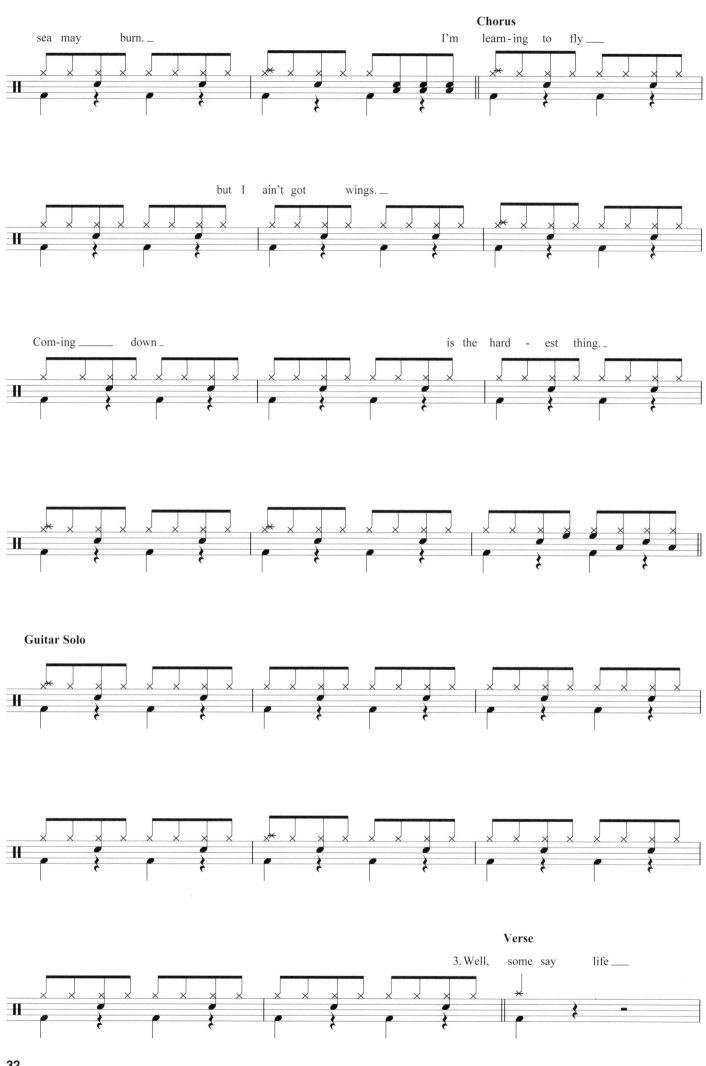

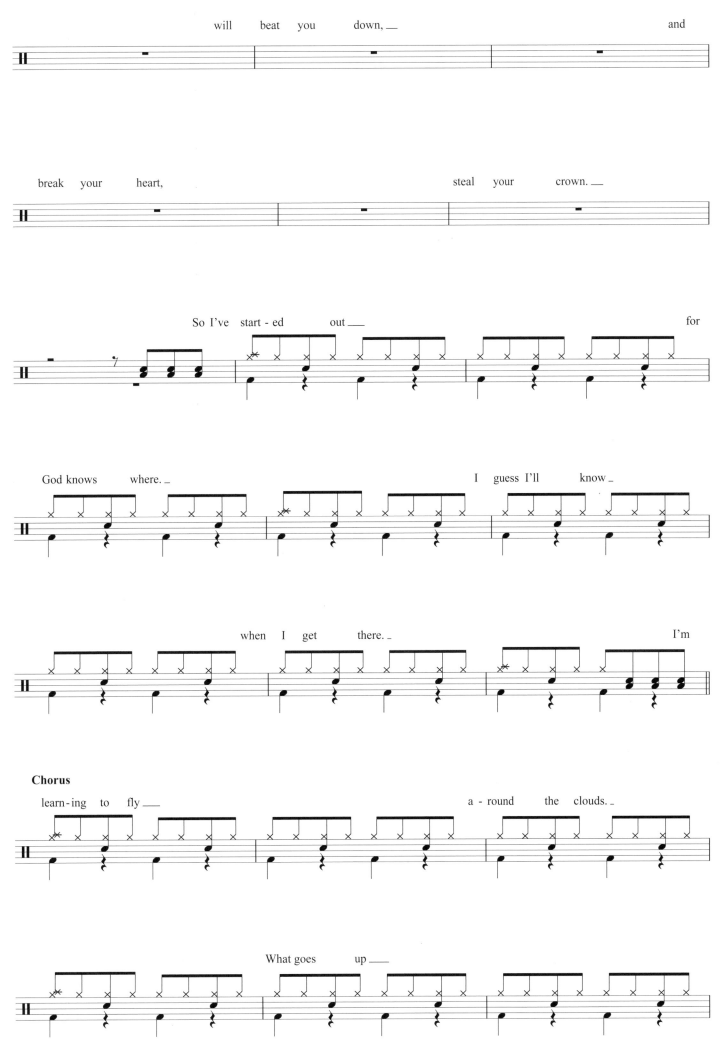

must come   down. _

Interlude

Ay!

Chorus

I'm   learn-ing to fly ___

but I ain't got   wings. _

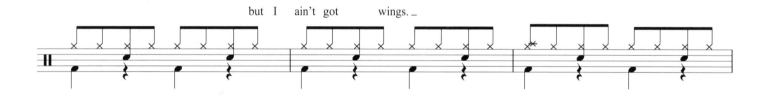

Com-ing _____ down _   is the hard - est thing. _

I'm learn-ing to fly ___   a -

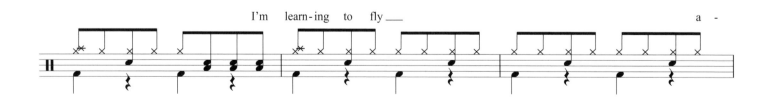

round   the clouds. _   And what goes   up ___

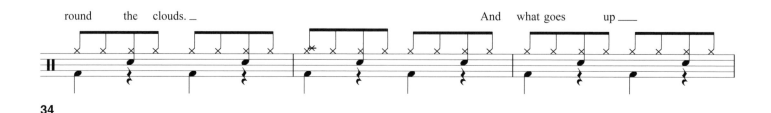

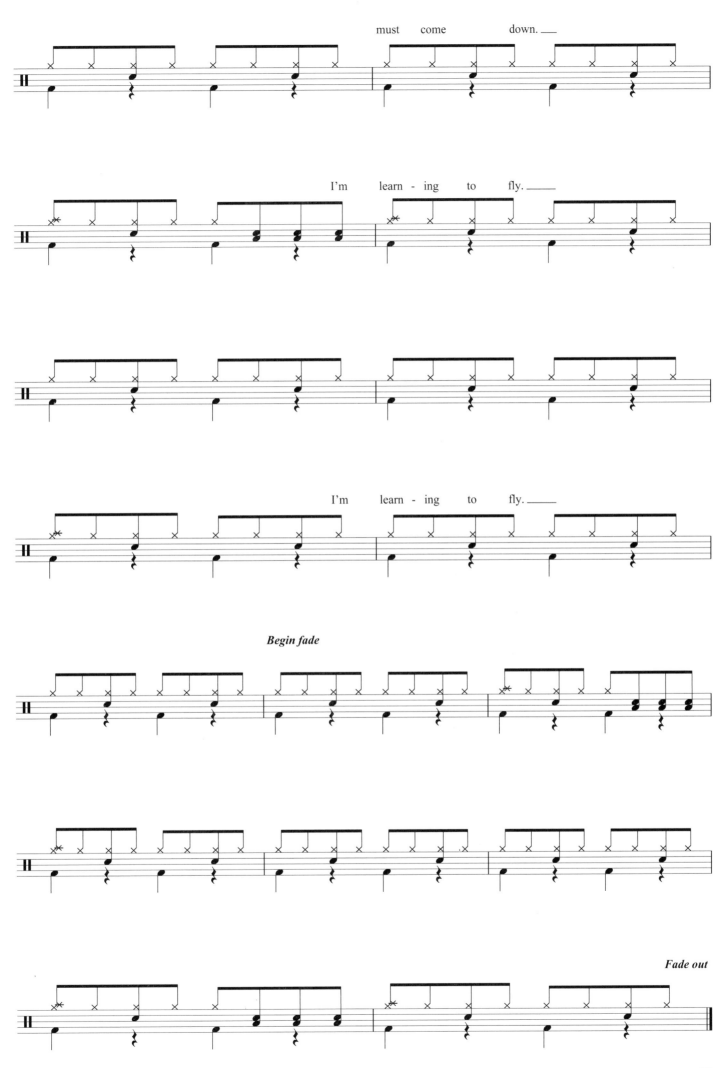

must come down. ____

I'm learn - ing to fly. ____

I'm learn - ing to fly. ____

Begin fade

Fade out

35

Seven Nation Army

Words and Music by Jack White

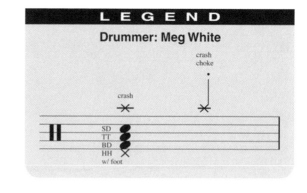

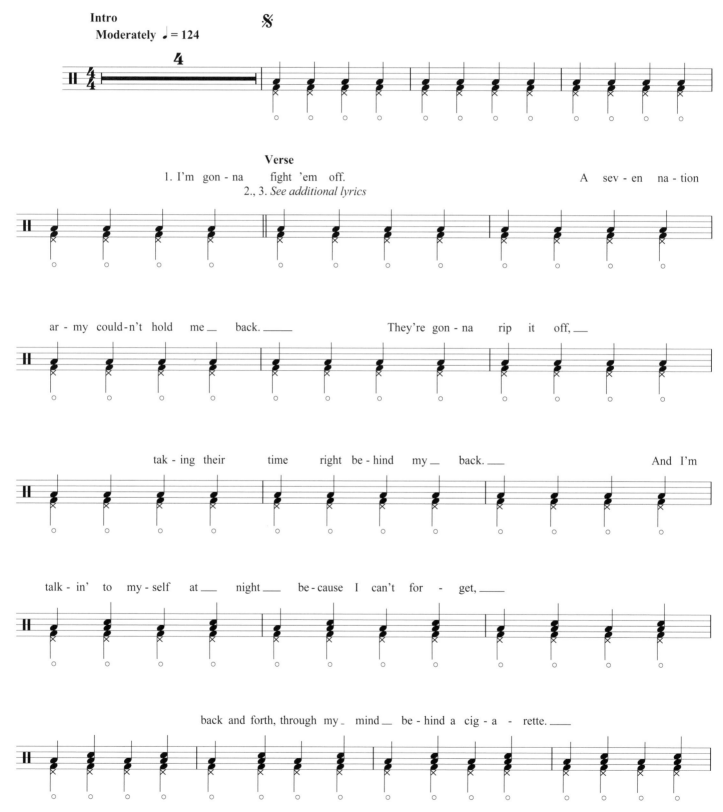

Additional Lyrics

2. Don't wanna hear about it,
   Ev'ry single one's got a story to tell.
   Ev'ry one knows about it
   From the Queen of England to the hounds of hell.
   And if I catch it comin' back my way
   I'm gonna serve it to you.
   And that ain't what you want to hear,
   But that's what I'll do.
   And the feeling coming from my bones says find a home.

3. I'm going to Wichita,
   Far from this opera forevermore.
   I'm gonna work the straw,
   Make the sweat drip out of every pore.
   And I'm bleeding, and I'm bleeding, and I'm
   Bleeding right before the Lord.
   All the words are gonna bleed from me
   And I will think no more.
   And the stains coming from my blood tell me go back home.

Sweet Home Alabama

Words and Music by Ronnie Van Zant, Ed King and Gary Rossington

Drummer: Bob Burns

Intro

Moderate Rock ♩ = 100

Verse

1. Big ___ wheels ___ keep on turn -

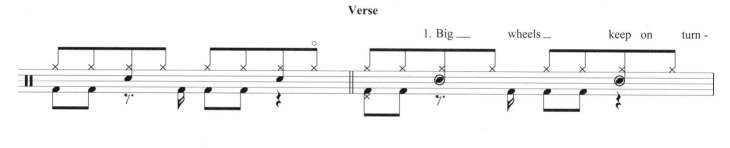

- in', car - ry me home to see my kin. ___

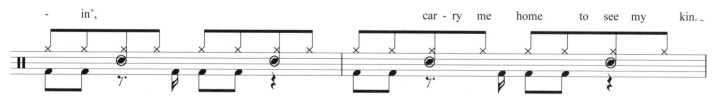

___ Sing - in' songs a - bout ___ the south -

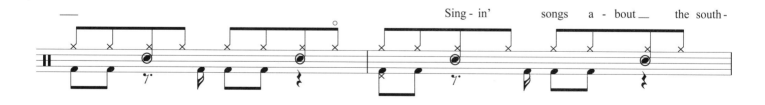

- land, I miss ole 'Bam - ee once a - gain ___

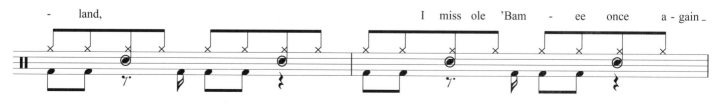

Sweet home Al - a - bam - a,

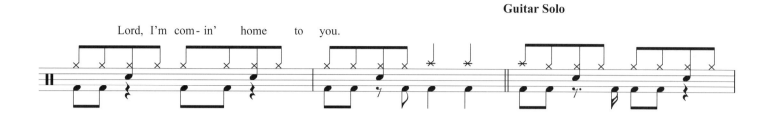

Lord, I'm com-in' home to you.

Guitar Solo

Verse

3. In Bir - ming - ham they love the gov - 'nor, boo, boo,

hoo. Now we all did what we could do.

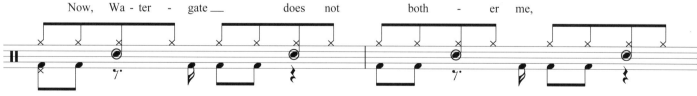

Now, Wa - ter - gate does not both - er me,

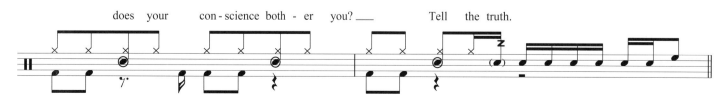

does your con-science both - er you? Tell the truth.

Chorus

Interlude

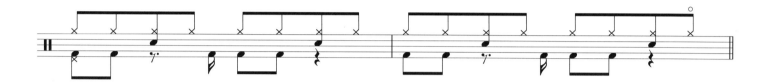

Verse

4. Now, Mus - cle   Shoals ___   has   got   the   Swamp ___   - ers,

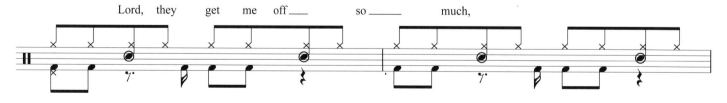

an' they   been   known ___   to   pick   a   song   or   two. ___

Lord,   they   get   me   off ___   so ___   much,

they   pick   me   up ___   when   I'm   feel - in'   blue, ___   'n' now   how 'bout   you?

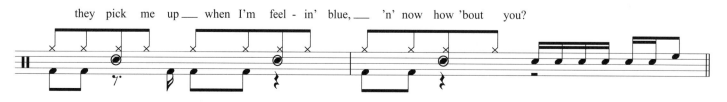

Chorus

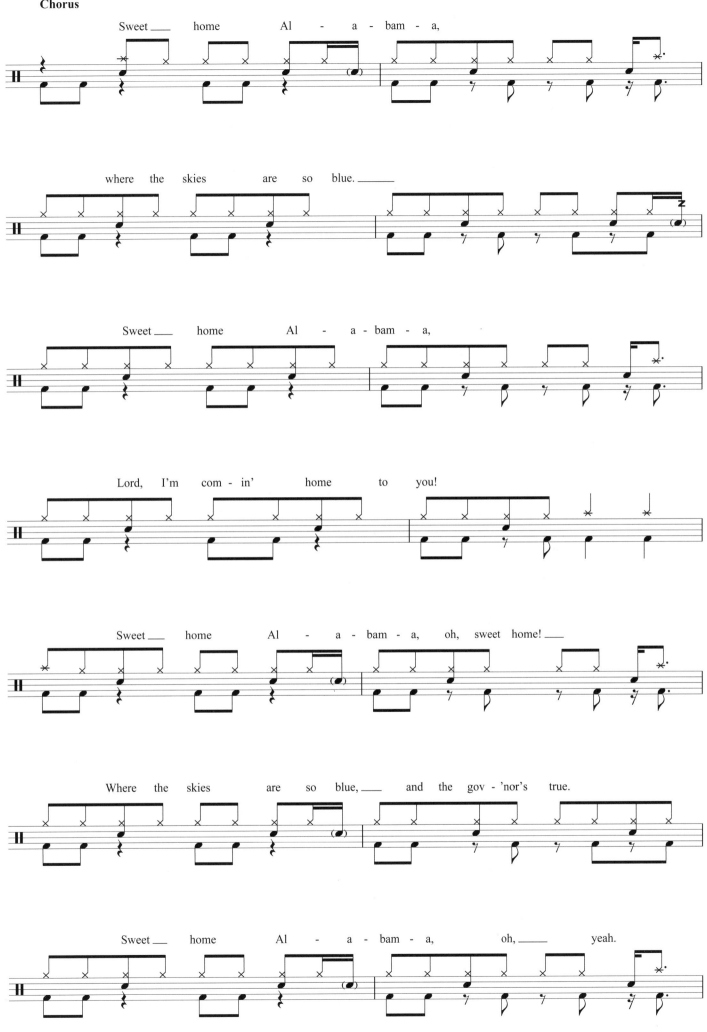

Lord, I'm com - in' home to you. Yeah. _____

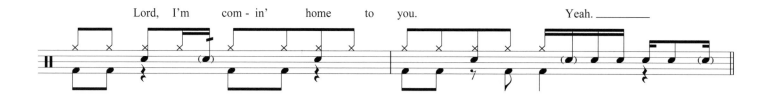

Outro

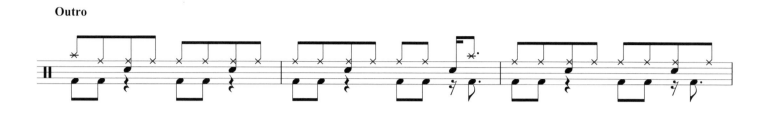

Begin fade

Fade out

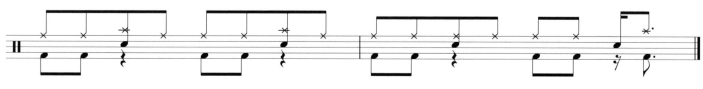

HAL•LEONARD® DRUM PLAY-ALONG

AUDIO ACCESS INCLUDED

The Drum Play-Along™ Series will help you play your favorite songs quickly and easily! Just follow the drum notation, listen to the audio to hear how the drums should sound, and then play-along using the separate backing tracks. The lyrics are also included for reference. The audio files are enhanced so you can adjust the recording to any tempo without changing pitch!

1. Pop/Rock
00699742.............................$14.99

2. Classic Rock
00699741.............................$15.99

3. Hard Rock
00699743.............................$15.99

4. Modern Rock
00699744.............................$15.99

5. Funk
00699745.............................$15.99

6. '90s Rock
00699746.............................$17.99

7. Punk Rock
00699747.............................$14.99

8. '80s Rock
00699832.............................$15.99

9. Cover Band Hits
00211599.............................$16.99

10. blink-182
00699834.............................$16.99

11. Jimi Hendrix Experience: Smash Hits
00699835.............................$17.99

12. The Police
00700268.............................$16.99

13. Steely Dan
00700202.............................$16.99

15. The Beatles
00256656.............................$16.99

16. Blues
00700272.............................$16.99

17. Nirvana
00700273.............................$15.99

18. Motown
00700274.............................$15.99

19. Rock Band: Modern Rock Edition
00700707.............................$17.99

20. Rock Band: Classic Rock Edition
00700708.............................$14.95

21. Weezer
00700959.............................$14.99

22. Black Sabbath
00701190.............................$16.99

23. The Who
00701191.............................$16.99

24. Pink Floyd – Dark Side of the Moon
00701612.............................$16.99

25. Bob Marley
00701703.............................$17.99

26. Aerosmith
00701887.............................$15.99

27. Modern Worship
00701921.............................$16.99

28. Avenged Sevenfold
00702388.............................$17.99

29. Queen
00702389.............................$16.99

30. Dream Theater
00111942.............................$24.99

31. Red Hot Chili Peppers
00702992.............................$19.99

32. Songs for Beginners
00704204.............................$14.99

33. James Brown
00117422.............................$16.99

34. U2
00124470.............................$16.99

35. Buddy Rich
00124640.............................$19.99

36. Wipe Out & 7 Other Fun Songs
00125341.............................$16.99

37. Slayer
00139861.............................$17.99

38. Eagles
00143920.............................$16.99

39. Kiss
00143937.............................$16.99

40. Stevie Ray Vaughan
00146155.............................$16.99

41. Rock Songs for Kids
00148113.............................$14.99

42. Easy Rock Songs
00148143.............................$14.99

45. Bon Jovi
00200891.............................$16.99

46. Mötley Crüe
00200892.............................$16.99

47. Metallica: 1983-1988
00234340.............................$19.99

48. Metallica: 1991-2016
00234341.............................$19.99

49. Top Rock Hits
00256655.............................$16.99

51. Deep Purple
00278400.............................$16.99

52. More Songs for Beginners
00278403.............................$14.99

53. Pop Songs for Kids
00298650.............................$15.99

HAL•LEONARD®

Visit Hal Leonard Online at
www.halleonard.com

DRUM TRANSCRIPTIONS
FROM HAL LEONARD

THE BEATLES DRUM COLLECTION

26 drum transcriptions of some of the Beatles' best, including: Back in the U.S.S.R. • Birthday • Can't Buy Me Love • Eight Days a Week • Help! • Helter Skelter • I Saw Her Standing There • Ob-La-Di, Ob-La-Da • Paperback Writer • Revolution • Sgt. Pepper's Lonely Hearts Club Band • Something • Twist and Shout • and more.

00690402 . . . .$19.99

BEST OF BLINK-182

Features Travis Barker's bashing beats from a baker's dozen of Blink's best. Songs: Adam's Song • Aliens Exist • All the Small Things • Anthem Part II • Dammit • Don't Leave Me • Dumpweed • First Date • Josie • Pathetic • The Rock Show • Stay Together for the Kids • What's My Age Again?

00690621 . . . .$19.99

DRUM CHART HITS

Authentic drum transcriptions of 30 pop and rock hits are including: Can't Stop the Feeling • Ex's & Oh's • Get Lucky • Moves like Jagger • Shake It Off • Thinking Out Loud • 24K Magic • Uptown Funk • and more.

00234062 . . . .$17.99

JIMI HENDRIX – ARE YOU EXPERIENCED?

This drum folio includes 17 transcriptions from this legendary album: Are You Experienced? • Fire • Foxey Lady • Hey Joe • Highway Chile • Love or Confusion • Manic Depression • May This Be Love • Purple Haze • Red House • Remember • Stone Free • Third Stone from the Sun • The Wind Cries Mary • more.

00690372 . . . .$16.99

INCUBUS DRUM COLLECTION

Drum transcriptions for 13 of the biggest hits from this alt-metal band. Includes: Are You In? • Blood on the Ground • Circles • A Crow Left of the Murder • Drive • Megalomaniac • Nice to Know You • Pardon Me • Privilege • Stellar • Talk Shows on Mute • Wish You Were Here • Zee Deveel.

00690763 . . . .$17.95

BEST OF THE DAVE MATTHEWS BAND FOR DRUMS

Cherry Lane Music

Note-for-note transcriptions of Carter Beauford's great drum work: The Best of What's Around • Crash into Me • What Would You Say.

02500184 . . . .$19.95

DAVE MATTHEWS BAND – FAN FAVORITES FOR DRUMS

Cherry Lane Music

Exact drum transcriptions of every Carter Beauford beat from 10 of the most requested DMB hits: Crush • Dancing Nancies • Everyday • Grey Street • Jimi Thing • The Space Between • Tripping Billies • Two Step • Warehouse • Where Are You Going.

02500643 . . . .$19.95

METALLICA – ...AND JUSTICE FOR ALL

Cherry Lane Music

Drum transcriptions to every song from Metallica's blockbuster album, plus complete drum setup diagrams, and background notes on Lars Ulrich's drumming style.

02503504 . . . .$19.99

METALLICA – BLACK

Cherry Lane Music

Matching folio to their critically acclaimed self-titled album. Includes: Enter Sandman * Sad But True * The Unforgiven * Don't Tread On Me * Of Wolf And Man * The God That Failed * Nothing Else Matters * and 5 more metal crunchers.

02503509 . . . .$19.99

METALLICA – MASTER OF PUPPETS

Cherry Lane Music

Matching folio to the best-selling album. Includes: Master Of Puppets • Battery • Leper Messiah • plus photos.

02503502 . . . .$19.99

METALLICA – RIDE THE LIGHTNING

Cherry Lane Music

Matching folio to Metallica's second album, including: Creeping Death • Fade To Black • and more.

02503507 . . . .$17.95

NIRVANA DRUM COLLECTION

Features transcriptions of Dave Grohl's actual drum tracks on 17 hits culled from four albums: *Bleach, Nevermind, Incesticide* and *In Utero*. Includes the songs: About a Girl • All Apologies • Blew • Come as You Are • Dumb • Heart Shaped Box • In Bloom • Lithium • (New Wave) Polly • Smells like Teen Spirit • and more. Also includes a drum notation legend.

00690316 . . . .$19.99

BEST OF RED HOT CHILI PEPPERS FOR DRUMS

Note-for-note drum transcriptions for every funky beat blasted by Chad Smith on 20 hits from *Mother's Milk* through *By the Way*! Includes: Aeroplane • Breaking the Girl • By the Way • Californication • Give It Away • Higher Ground • Knock Me Down • Me and My Friends • My Friends • Right on Time • Scar Tissue • Throw Away Your Television • True Men Don't Kill Coyotes • Under the Bridge • and more.

00690587 . . . .$22.99

RED HOT CHILI PEPPERS – GREATEST HITS

Essential for Peppers fans! Features Chad Smith's thunderous drumming transcribed note-for-note from their *Greatest Hits* album. 15 songs: Breaking the Girl • By the Way • Californication • Give It Away • Higher Ground • My Friends • Scar Tissue • Suck My Kiss • Under the Bridge • and more.

00690681 . . . .$19.99

RED HOT CHILI PEPPERS – I'M WITH YOU

Note-for-note drum transcriptions from the group's tenth album: The Adventures of Rain Dance Maggie • Annie Wants a Baby • Brendan's Death Song • Dance, Dance, Dance • Did I Let You Know • Ethiopia • Even You Brutus? • Factory of Faith • Goodbye Hooray • Happiness Loves Company • Look Around • Meet Me at the Corner • Monarchy of Roses • Police Station.

00691168 . . . .$22.99

RUSH – THE SPIRIT OF RADIO: GREATEST HITS 1974-1987

17 exact drum transcriptions from Neil Peart! Includes: Closer to the Heart • Fly by Night • Freewill • Limelight • Red Barchetta • Spirit of Radio • Subdivisions • Time Stand Still • Tom Sawyer • The Trees • Working Man • 2112 (I Overture & II Temples of Syrinx).

00323857 . . . .$22.99

HAL•LEONARD®

7777 W. BLUEMOUND RD. P.O. BOX 13819 MILWAUKEE, WI 53213

www.halleonard.com

Prices, contents and availability subject to change without notice.

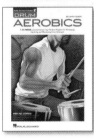